T0208012

HERE COMES THE GROOM

Will You Be Ready For Christ's Return?

ANGELA HIGGS

WESTBOW
PRESS®
A DIVISION OF THOMAS NELSON
& ZONDERVAN

WestBow Press books may be ordered through
booksellers or by contacting:

WestBow Press
A Division of Thomas Nelson & Zondervan
1663 Liberty Drive
Bloomington, IN 47403
www.westbowpress.com
844-714-3454

ISBN: 978-1-6642-7325-2 (sc)
ISBN: 978-1-6642-7326-9 (e)

Library of Congress Control Number: 2022913431

Print information available on the last page.

WestBow Press rev. date: 07/26/2022

INTRODUCTION

Let us rejoice and be glad and give Him glory! For the wedding of the Lamb has come, and His bride has made herself ready. Fine linen, bright and clean, was given her to wear. Then the angel said to me, "Write this: Blessed are those who are invited to the wedding supper of the Lamb!" And then he added, "These are the true words of God." (Revelation 19:7, 8 NIV; *fine linen* stands for the righteous acts of God's holy people)

How does a bride make herself ready? How does she prepare herself for the wedding? How does it all come together? We all know how this typically works. Even in our modern day, some things really do remain traditional in this sense. The dating relationship is where it all begins. Dating relationships are a two-way pursuit. We have all seen enough movies, TV shows, social media posts, and the always charming baseball stadium proposals—and some of us even have our own personal experience—to know that the man will be the one to declare, "This is the one whom I love. This is the one I wish to spend the rest of my life with. This is the one whose hand I would like to ask for in marriage." It is the groom-to-be who does the asking with the question "Will you marry me?"

A whole lot of preparation is already in place on his side of this event. He has most likely already picked out a ring and chosen a location that will be somewhat romantic, meaningful, and memorable. I cannot even imagine all the pressure he must face to make this special occasion be so moving in his potential bride's heart. If we factor in the pressures of today's world and all the social media platforms, it's over the top. Many people hire professional photographers and cinematographers to capture such an intimate moment. Others may at least be sure that a friend or family member is there to hold a steady hand while recording with an ordinary cell phone. Yes, marriage proposals have always been a pretty big deal. An even bigger deal is the shift that occurs the very moment that the delighted bride gushes an overjoyed "Yes!"

The mysterious shift that takes place is called the engagement. The dating couple now become the engaged couple. The terms "girlfriend" and "boyfriend" have graduated to something much more sophisticated: a woman becomes a fiancée, and a man becomes a fiancé. (He just gets one *e*, according to French spelling conventions.)

I happen to have firsthand experience with the engagement period. I've been a delighted bride making all the preparations, choosing the right location, selecting the caterer, picking out the most beautiful music, and (don't forget!) the invitations. The most fun part, of course, is trying on all the wedding dresses! But while it can be fun, it can also be a bit overwhelming. I was a young bride by today's standards. I was young even in my generation. When my groom asked me to be his bride, it was an instant and excited "Yes!" We were so lucky to have both sets of parents give their immediate blessings. My parents were gaining a son, and his parents were gaining a daughter. Given that I was my mom and dad's only daughter, my parents very much enjoyed and devoted themselves to wedding preparations every step of the way, and they were right alongside me in every detail of planning this life changing event. They were a constant source of encouragement as we moved closer to the big day. A wedding would take place, a celebration would be had, and ultimately a godly marriage would be established. It's all quite simple in our culture today, compared to ancient Israel.

We will get to those details later, but for now let's turn our attention to an upcoming event that will take place in the courts of Heaven. The Bible refers to this event as the marriage supper of the Lamb. You may not have heard of this event as told in the Bible, but it will be the most over-the-top event in the history of the world. The most wonderful venue could never compare to this wedding feast.

In the Bible, the church is affectionately referred to as the Bride of Christ. I admit that this does sound a little strange, like something out of a Dark Age fairy tale. Just who is this "bride" that the Bible speaks of, and what are the details of this wedding feast to come? When the Bible talks about this bride, it is not referring to the major and minor prophets, nor to Adam and Eve, Noah and all the animals on the ark, Father Abraham, Queen Esther, Moses, King David, King Solomon, or even Daniel from the lion's den. Don't misunderstand: these mighty men and women of valor most definitely will be at this magnificent wedding feast. After all, they played such an important role as they walked out their faith and devotion to the Lord in order to bring about the promised one, the Messiah, the Bridegroom Jesus.

As we discover all the wedding guests, you may recognize some of these names, even if you are reaching all the way back to vacation Bible school. You may not have a plethora of Bible knowledge, but I think you will keep up just fine.

1

THE GUEST LIST

Wouldn't you just love to sit next to Adam and Eve? I sure would! I'd love to ask, "Why did you do it? Why did you eat of the forbidden fruit?" (We'll get to that later on.) I'd also love to sit at the table with Abraham and Sarah, who left their country and their family to go to an unknown land after God spoke to Abraham directing him to do so. God promised them that they would have a child even though Sarah had been barren and was well past childbearing age. She didn't believe God, so she took matters into her own hands and gave Abraham her handmaiden Hagar to conceive a child with. As you can imagine, that didn't go so well. In between taking bites of wedding cake, I would love to ask her what she was thinking when she decided that would be the answer to their dilemma! But as God did promise, eventually the promised seed was born to Sarah.

Next we have their promised son, Isaac, at our table. I would like to hear Isaac's side of the story when he realized that his father, Abraham, was taking him to Mount Moriah to be sacrificed at the Lord's instruction. Oh, the relief they both must have felt when the Lord stopped Abraham and provided a ram in the thicket to sacrifice instead. That was a close one!

What about Rebekah, the wife of Isaac? How did she know that he was the right one to leave her family for, marrying someone she had never even met? Later, how did Rebekah feel when God told her there were two babies inside her womb that would bring about two nations?

I would also love to stop by the table of Jacob and listen in on that dinner conversation. I wonder whom Jacob will sit by? Will he sit by Rachel, the beautiful wife he loved, or by his other wife Leah, Rachel's "weak-eyed" sister whom Jacob was tricked by their father into marrying first? (That's how the Bible refers to her—"weak-eyed.") Their father, Laban, figured this was the only way he could marry off his unattractive daughter. Well, I am glad that they all did tie the knot, because between the two wives, along with their handmaidens, they gained twelve sons and acquired the twelve tribes of Israel.

One of those sons was Joseph, who was the son of Jacob's beloved wife Rachael. I would want to ask him how he forgave his brothers, the sons of Leah, who were jealous of him and sold him into slavery, and then faked his death. While in slavery, he remained faithful to God. The Bible says he was so very handsome, and that is the reason that Potiphar's wife would just not leave him alone. She tried her best to get him to succumb to temptation. When she realized he would not sin against God or betray his master Potiphar in that way, she accused him of just the opposite. He was falsely accused and thrown into a dungeon. While there, he remained faithful to God, making the best of the bad situation. God had given him the gift of correctly interpreting others' dreams, and he did so during his imprisonment.

After one of his fellow prisoners was released, he started telling of the man who had this gift. As word got around, Joseph was summoned by the pharaoh to interpret his own dream. Joseph was spot-on in predicting a severe famine to come upon the land. He was able to save the people by warning them to store up provisions and was placed second in command of all Egypt.

While he was in this position of great authority, Joseph's brothers came to seek help during the famine. They did not recognize their brother, who they believed to be enslaved. Can you imagine the revenge he could have taken on his brothers in this place of authority? But when he revealed himself to his brothers, he forgave them. I'm glad he did, because he demonstrated how a dysfunctional family can become functional. God had a plan. He saved his people from famine.

Now, let's look around for some other important

guests. I'm sure we will be able to spot Moses in the crowd of Israelites. Maybe the crowd of dinner guests will be parted down the middle in order to see him. Remember how the Lord parted the Red Sea so that the Israelites could be led out of captivity under Pharaoh's rule? They were led to wander in the dessert for forty years on their way to the promised land. Moses never did quite make it there, but I'm glad he will be a part of this wedding feast.

What about Ruth? Will she still be hanging around with her mother-in-law, Naomi? After all, when they were both widowed, Ruth did pledge to her "Where you go, I will go." That pledge to follow Naomi led her straight into the arms of Boaz, her kinsman redeemer, and also into the lineage of Christ. Together Ruth and Boaz had a son, Obed. Through Obed, we get to Jesse, who is the father of another special wedding guest. This guest just may be in charge of music coordinating at the wedding reception. He might even be playing the harp. I am certain we can at least see him dancing before the Lord. Yes, you've guessed it: King David, known as the man after God's own heart.

David was anointed to be king while he was just a young shepherd boy. Nothing seemingly special about him. He was special, though, when he slew the giant Goliath with just a slingshot and a small stone. He was a bit intolerant of anyone who came against the name of the Lord. Was he perfect? Not even close. He did fall into sin with Bathsheba by committing adultery with her, and had her husband killed by putting him on the front lines of battle in wartime. Uh, a "man after God's own heart"? How? Well, King David was sorry for his sin and had a repentant heart. He sought the Lord's heart above all else. We could all sit down at his table and take note of how to seek the Lord's heart above all.

The place will be filled with all these wonderful personas we've only read about. It will be so exciting to recognize all these heroes of the faith. We can't forget about Mary, the mother of our Lord. I want to know how excited or fearful she was when the angel Gabriel approached her about the Holy Spirit coming upon her to conceive the Savior of the world. I would thank her for her lovely response: "Behold the maidservant of the Lord. Let it be to me according to your word" (Luke 1:38 NKJV). She was a willing vessel.

In the Bible, there is a long list of key people God used to play out the plans he had. In the lineage of generations that would usher in the promised one, we come to Jesus, Yeshua in Hebrew. The genealogy of Jesus is filled with riveting stories and people with God-given purposes leading toward this Jewish messiah.

So what does any of this talk have to do with weddings? Good question! I will try and answer this the very best I can. I'm sure there is some room for error on my part. Anyone can search for the answers. You do not need to have a theology degree—in fact, you don't even need to have attended one day of college. You do, however, need a Bible. You have to read it. I have read it cover to cover. I am not an expert on it, but as I write this, I have been a student of God's Word for twenty-six years. I won't do this topic justice, but I love this topic because it has brought justice to me.

> Therefore, having been justified by faith, we have peace with God though our Lord Jesus Christ. (Romans 5:1 NKJV)

Now let's go back in time. Way back. Back to a garden ... the garden of Eden.

2

THE FIRST COUPLE

I n Genesis, we read that God created the heavens and the earth. He began creating all the wonderful things we need and use every day. Light, dark, evening, morning, the sky, the sea, every living thing in the water, every living creature and animal according to their kind. He called it all "good."

But God didn't stop there. He kept on creating. He said, "Let us make man in Our image" (Genesis 1:26 NKJV). He then created man in His own image. The Lord planted a beautiful and lush garden for man, a complete paradise. And then the Lord God said, "It is not good for man to be alone; I will make him a helper comparable to him" (Genesis 2:18 NKJV). Out of all creation, and all the animals the Lord God had formed, there was no suitable helper. So God caused a deep sleep to come over Adam. While Adam slept, He took one of Adam's ribs from him and formed a woman. This is the part where we meet the woman. Behold Eve!

> And the Lord God caused a deep sleep to fall on Adam, and he slept; and He took one of his ribs and closed up the flesh in its place. Then the rib which the Lord God had taken from man he made into a woman, and He brought her to the man. And Adam said: "This is now bone of my bones and flesh of my flesh; She shall be called Woman, because she was taken out of Man." (Genesis 2:21–23 NKJV)

Man was created in total perfection by the Lord Himself. It seems as if everything will be just fine, and they will live in a garden of paradise forever. Adam and his wife were both naked and unashamed, becoming one flesh in all their spare time. They only had to live in this beautiful garden with a beautiful flow of water to gaze at. No worries, no troubles, no death, no loss, and ultimately no sin. They also got to enjoy all the delicious, ripe, and lovely fruit. Well … almost all the delicious, ripe, and lovely fruit. There was that one tree. The Tree of the Knowledge of Good and Evil. The Lord God instructed the man and his wife never to eat of its fruit or surely they would die. Seems easy enough, right? Enjoy the fruit from the tree of life and continue to live in this peaceful Shangri-la, or eat the fruit from the Tree of Knowledge of Good and Evil and die. Got it! Sounds like an easy choice to me.

Well, as it turns out, it wasn't such an easy choice for Eve—especially when that crafty serpent, Satan, came along and asked Eve a simple question: "Has God indeed said, 'You shall not eat of any tree of the garden'?" (Genesis 3:1 NKJV). She cleared that misunderstanding up right away by telling him what we read next.

> And the woman said to the serpent, "We may eat the fruit of the trees of the garden, but of the fruit of the tree which is in the midst of the garden, God has said, 'You shall not eat it, nor shall you touch it, lest you die.'" (Genesis 3:2–3 NKJV)

Good job, Eve; set him straight.

But the serpent continued his usual trickery and deception.

> Then the serpent said to the woman, "You will not surely die. For God knows that in the day you eat of it your eyes will be opened, and you will be like God, knowing good and evil." (Genesis 3:4–5 NKJV)

It seems as though Eve was afraid God was keeping something from her. Then she saw the fruit and how pleasing to the eye it was. She took it, and she ate it. And then she gave some to Adam, her husband, who also willingly partook. It was just that easy to disobey the Lord. One temptation, one time, one bite.

That bite plunged all of humanity into opposition with a perfect God. They sinned. They were suddenly aware that they were naked. They felt ashamed for the first time. They sewed fig leaves together to cover themselves. From then on everything changed. They had to toil for their food, working it from the ground now instead of just conveniently pulling it off trees. They even had to wear clothes from then on.

Adam and Eve, our first couple, were cast out of the garden, and now great pain would come to Eve with childbirth. Well, not just Eve, but every other woman who has been through birthing a child. Now they would know what death is. Now we all do.

I'm not happy about their choice. This has affected me personally in more ways than I could count. Hasn't it affected you too? Now we are all born into this fallen world that is eventually going to be infected with the natural process of death. Now we are all born by default into a sinful nature. The apostle Paul's letter to the Romans (3:23 NIV) says "all have sinned and have fallen short of the glory of God." Yes, all. That means you, and that means me. But verse 24 goes on to say that we "are justified freely by his grace through the redemption that came by Christ Jesus."

Don't think that the crafty serpent gets off so easy either. He will have his day. See, Jesus had a plan even at that very moment, the plan of redemption for us. It was going to cost Him something though. It was going to cost His life.

3

SACRIFICE AND THE SAVIOR

For God so loved the world that he gave his one and only son, that whoever believes in him shall not parish but have eternal life. For God did not send his Son into the world to condemn the world, but to save the world through him. (John 3:16–17 NIV)

This whole Adam and Eve thing sounds pretty hopeless, doesn't it? Like we are all complete victims of sin and must endure all the consequences brought on by the first couple. If you think that, then you are right. It's true. It really is a hopeless situation. That's why in the Old Testament we see so many imperfect people who sin. However, when they sinned and broke God's law in the Old Testament, He provided a very detailed way to have their sin atoned for: animal sacrifice.

Now, this may raise some animal rights activists' eyebrows. But the one who broke God's law with sin would have to present to a high priest a perfect and unblemished free bull, goat, sheep, ram, or any member of the animal kingdom considered acceptable, offering it in order to be cleared of their sin. An animal would be slaughtered, and blood would have to be shed.

However, we don't have to do that anymore. Just as the "Old Man," Adam, brought sin into the world, causing death, the "New Man," Jesus Christ, brought with Him redemption that brings life. He became the all-time sacrifice for us. It was His blood that did our clearing. This is good news! God promised the very moment sin entered into the world to make a way of redemption through his son, Jesus Christ. It just happened to take about four thousand years to get to the long-awaited Messiah.

> For unto us a child is born, unto us a Son is given; And the government will rest on His shoulders; And His Name will be called Wonderful, Councilor, Mighty God, Everlasting Father, Prince of Peace. (Isaiah 9:6 NIV)

Throughout the Bible, it has been prophesied that all Israel would receive their messiah. To this day they are still waiting. A good reminder to them might be found in the Old Testament book of Isaiah.

> Who has believed our report? And to whom has the arm of the Lord been revealed? For He shall grow up before Him as a tender plant, And as a root out of dry ground. He has no form or comeliness; And when we see Him, there is no beauty that we should desire Him. He is despised and rejected by men, A Man of sorrows and acquainted with grief. And we hid, as it were, our faces from Him. Surely, He has borne our griefs and carried our sorrows; Yet we esteemed Him stricken, Smitten by God, and afflicted. But He was wounded for our transgressions, He was bruised for our iniquities' The chastisement for our peace was upon Him, And by His stripes we are healed. (Isaiah 53:1–5 NKJV)

You see, Jesus did come. You probably know the Christmas story. He was born of a virgin, Mary, who lived among His chosen people. He performed His first miracle when He turned the water into wine at the wedding in Cana. He healed blind eyes, He opened deaf ears, He cleansed leprosy that plagued the outcasts. He also healed crippled people who had never walked their entire lives. Jesus also cast out demons that were tormenting people. He raised the dead for all to see.

He also did something very scandalous: He dined with known sinners, such as tax collectors, prostitutes, and outcasts. This was something the religious leaders took special note of and frowned on. In their minds, He just didn't fit the description of the long-awaited messiah they expected. They were especially outraged when he healed on the Sabbath.

This takes us to the Easter story. You know the holiday that fills our stores today with silly-looking chocolate bunnies, fake grass, baby marshmallow chicks, messy egg-dying kits, and (my personal *least* favorite) jelly beans. Yuck! (I will take all the chocolate bunnies, though.) The real Easter story is how Jesus willingly went to the cross to be the one-time perfect sacrifice for our sin. The sacrifices of bulls, goats, sheep, rams were done away with. Jesus is the perfect Lamb whose shed blood covers our sin. He paid a high price for all of mankind—for the Jew, and also the Gentile.

Did you realize that Jesus was Jewish, born from all-Jewish lineage? He came to save the lost sheep of Israel. But they rejected him, as they were blinded by their one ideal of what a messiah would be. Even today, He is still in pursuit of their precious hearts as His chosen people.

So where does "the church" come in? "The church" refers collectively to those who have put their faith in the person of Jesus Christ and made Him their Lord and their Savior. Does this mean that the church has simply replaced Israel? Not at all. The Bible is clear on this.

The Bible uses the illustration of a tree, as the apostle Paul, also a Jew, explains it to the followers of Jesus in the early church:

> If the first piece of dough is holy, the lump is also; and if the root is holy, the branches are too. But if some of the branches were broken off, and you, being a wild olive, were grafted in among them and became partaker with them of the rich root of the olive tree, do not be arrogant toward the branches; but if you are arrogant, remember that it is not you who supports the root, but the root supports you. You will say then, "Branches were broken off so that I might be grafted in." Quite right, they were broken off for their unbelief, but you stand by your faith. Do not be conceited, but fear: for if God did not spare the natural branches, He will not spare you either. Behold then the kindness and severity of God; to those who fell, severity, but to you, God's kindness, if you continue in His kindness; otherwise, you also will be cut off. And they also, if they do not continue in their unbelief, will be grafted in, for God is able to

graft them in again. For if you were cut off from what is by nature a wild olive tree, and were grafted contrary to nature into a cultivated olive tree, how much more will these who are the natural branches be grafted into their own olive tree? For I do not want you, brethren to be uninformed of the mystery-so that you will not be wise in your own estimation-that a partial hardening has happened to Israel until the fullness of the gentiles has come in; and so all Israel will be saved; just as it is written,

"THE DELIVERER WILL COME FROM ZION, HE WILL REMOVE UNGODLINESS FROM JACOB. THIS IS MY COVENANT WITH THEM, WHEN I TAKE AWAY THEIR SINS." (Romans 11:16–27 NASB)

Paul is trying to get across the point that the church, although special, has not replaced His chosen people. Israel is the root of this tree; the church is a special grafted-in branch. We are wild. With God's very own skilled hands, He has grafted us into the tree.

I grew up in a church that strongly recognized this and deeply valued the Jewish origin of the Christian faith. It has a very special place in the hearts of my family. Some simply overlook this truth. In Genesis, God established the covenant with Abraham, saying,

"I will bless those who bless you, and whoever curses you I will curse; and all peoples on earth will be blessed through you" (Genesis 12:3 NIV). That is a very good reason to hold the Jewish people in high esteem. You don't have to tell me twice!

There may even be Christians who have never thought to bless the Jewish people or pray for their peace. If that is you, no need to feel condemned, just begin to do so now.

4

THE WEDDINGS OF ANCIENT ISRAEL

In comparison with the wedding planning of ancient Israel, our wedding planning customs are actually quite simple, mundane, and even robotic.

In ancient Israel wedding custom, we find a very different procedure in how a wedding banquet comes together. When a young man was in pursuit of a bride, he would go directly to her father's house and have a little talk with him. It does seem all business, but deep down under the surface, I think it is just a tiny bit romantic—even if in some cases this engagement was arranged by their families. You would really have to trust your parents match making skills here.

The would-be groom brought a legal agreement to present to the father, with the price he was willing to pay in exchange for the bride. This is referred to as "the bride price." Back then, a man with daughters was sort of at a disadvantage. It meant that the family might not have as many strong, able-bodied sons to help in their survival, providing labor and increasing funds for living. Daughters simply had a different role back then, and I'm OK with that. The daughter's value surfaced when the potential bridegroom was willing to pay up. If her father approved of the groom and the price he was willing to pay, he would then invite the potential bride to the table, and in most cases, she could then decide if she was a willing vessel to make a covenant contract with the groom. If she agreed, then the deal was sealed and the contract went into effect. This was basically their marriage license. A legally binding agreement. A covenant.

Should she decide to opt in and become his bride, were they able to run off immediately as husband and wife and begin honeymooning at a resort near the Mediterranean Sea? Not exactly. She then had to bid farewell to her bridegroom and enter into a waiting period of up to a year. Can't you just imagine this goodbye playing out like a scene on a big movie screen? Maybe they were able to have a moment and embrace in a long, passionate, heart-pounding goodbye kiss. Maybe the handsome groom would look upon his beautiful bride, and in the one-liner way of a movie scene declare, "I will be back for you, my love." Then he'd swing from a rope off her balcony, drop to the ground, and scurry off into the night. I could see that happening.

Now that she was spoken for, from that point she

would wear a veil over her face every time she went out in public, which communicated to the world that she was spoken for—a lot like the engagement rings brides wear today. This veil separated her from the world as she declared that she belonged to someone else. She belonged to her bridegroom only.

OK, you may be wondering why her groom would leave her. Why didn't he stick around? Is he the wandering type? The answer is that he simply had to go back to his father's house and build a bridal chamber. His one desire was to make sure that it would be a place where he can love her and cherish her.

Now, that is beginning to sound a lot like a New Testament scripture I've read in the book of John:

> My Father's house has many rooms; if that were not so, would I have told you that I am going there to prepare a place for you? And if I go and prepare a place for you, I will come back and take you to be with me that you also may be where I am. You know the way to the place where I am going. (John 14:3–4 NIV)

It sounds so obsolete, but yes, he had to prepare a special place to return to with his bride. He wanted it to be special and exactly to her liking, to make sure it would suit her every need. This would be a special place where they would begin their wedding celebration.

While waiting for her bridegroom to return for her,

the bride has some preparing of her own to do. She really would have no idea when he might be back for her. It could be any night now. "Could it be tonight?" she wonders. "Could it be six months from now?" she second-guesses. If he tarries for long, she may begin to get frustrated or even fearful. "Did he forget about me?" she may fret. "Did he find someone else?" she may wonder. "Should I find someone else?"

If these thoughts plague her mind, all she must do is go and look at the agreement they made together. She needs to be reminded by the covenant she entered into with him. This settles her mind and reassures her that he will return. For those of us who are believers, our covenant reminder is reading the Bible.

As she continues to make preparation, she is only focused on her groom. She thinks of him often. She needs to be prepared to go with him whenever he returns for her. How exciting this must have been! She will need her bridal clothes ready; she will also need her bridal attendants ready. Her bridesmaids need to be as ready as she is.

Another very important item that needs to be in place is her oil lamp, since it was custom for the groom to return at the midnight hour. Ancient Israel did not have electricity—no streetlights, no motion sensor on the front porch or garage door. They relied on fire for their lighting. The oil lamp could burn only as long as there was oil in it. If the bride's oil was low, she would not be able to find her way.

When the time finally came, the bridegroom was

all set to go and romantically steal his bride away in the night. As he and his groomsmen came near her home, they let out a shout. This shout was their fair warning that the time was approaching, and he would soon be in her presence to take her away with him. As the bridal procession then went to where he had prepared a place for her and arranged the marriage supper, onlookers would watch and cheer along with the whole wedding party. What a celebration!

This is a beautiful portrayal of what a pledge of love and loyalty looks like. As soon as they got to the destination, all the wedding guests would begin the celebration, while the bride and groom privately entered the marriage bed and consummated their marriage. The couple would spend the next seven days here alone together while the celebration was going on. Imagine the intimacy taking place while they were finally getting to truly know each other. They got their fill of knowing each other physically, emotionally, and spiritually. No distractions, and locked away from the world. Only the two of them becoming one flesh.

> Therefore, a man shall leave his father and mother and be joined to his wife, and they shall become one flesh. (Genesis 2:24 NIV)

Now, let's try to understand why in the New Testament Jesus Himself uses the ancient wedding of Israel as his reference when he addresses the church. It's a true love story. A story of faithful love, devotion, and enduring promise. It is the rescue that our hearts desire. We are all born into this very story. Just as we learned that we are born in sin through the story of Adam and Eve's fall, we are also reborn into love through Jesus's pursuit of sinners. The Bible says that Jesus, our Bridegroom, is coming back for the bride, the church. That's us! We as believers are the bride.

It's not association or affiliation with any church or denomination that makes us the bride, nor whether someone in your family is a professing Christian, be it your husband, wife, mom, dad, son, daughter, grandchild, or grandparent. Those associations will not save you. This is personal. As Jesus declared to Nicodemus, "Very truly I tell you, no one can see the kingdom of God unless they are born again" (John 3:3 NIV). Anyone who has placed their faith in the Lord Jesus Christ and made Him their Lord and declared Him their savior, repented of their sin, and entered into a personal relationship with Him has been born again and now has the highly honored title of "bride." This special title is given regardless of existing relationship titles such as man, woman, husband, wife, daughter, son, mother, father, grandfather, grandmother, aunt, uncle, brother, sister, cousin, niece, nephew, neighbor, or friend. All believers are now simply known as the church, the bride of Christ.

What does the bride look like? Let me just say that this bride is not perfect. She has many imperfections. To be honest, some of her can be just plain and unattractive.

I have often wondered if this bride is even worthy of the pursuit of her Bridegroom Jesus. Thankfully, He sees her true beauty. Jesus is the bride's ultimate beauty treatment. He is the one who has placed value in her. He is the one who can make all of us into something beautiful.

5

THE WEDDING PLANNER

My first job was working in a bridal boutique as a bridal consultant. I sold wedding dresses. It sounds very glamorous. I also thought it sounded glamorous. I thought it would be six days a week, working in an elegant atmosphere with beautiful, lavish wedding gowns and delighted brides-to-be gracefully shopping while their mannerly friends and family members displayed royal etiquette. Well, it didn't take me long at all to learn that it would in fact sometimes be the complete opposite of all those lovely images I had conjured up in my mind.

Most brides-to-be enter into the bridal gown shopping experience sort of detached from what will take place. More often than not, a bride comes into the boutique not really knowing what kind of exposure that is about to take place. Maybe she didn't get the memo that she will be going into a dressing room not by herself but with the attendant, a total stranger, sometimes two, to get dressed down to the bare essentials. She doesn't really know that putting on those expensive, heavily beaded or sequined, satin or silk embroidered gowns will be a two-person job. The gown must be lifted over her or be pushed down while she will need assistance for stepping into it.

That's where I'd come in. At your service! Let's get this dress sold! In my time working there, let's just say … I've seen some things. I've seen some things on the surface, and some things perhaps on a deeper level. I list all these things not from a critical viewpoint, but more just as observations, which I believe correlate with the imperfect bride that Jesus is preparing for Himself.

OK, let's go into the dressing room. The dressing room is always a vulnerable place—a place where you expect to be alone to observe yourself in the mirror. When trying on wedding dresses, however, suddenly you realize that you are not alone under the harsh lighting, fully exposed to your own reflection. There is an extra pair of eyes, or even two pairs, scanning those imperfections that you would rather not show. And once you are in there, it's too late. You are exposed. But it shouldn't take too long for the bride to realize that the bridal consultants are on her side. They want to cover flaws artfully and accentuate and beautify the very best of the bride. There are no brides-to-be who come into the dressing room already the epitome of perfection.

The things I recall are not meant as criticisms but more like a roll call of realities.

I've seen some really bad, orange, streaky fake tans.

I've seen some of the palest legs that looked as though they've never seen the sun. I needed sunglasses due to the glare of light reflecting off those legs.

I've seen some weird tattoos. Back before they were a cultural norm, they were more hidden.

I've seen very worn-out and ratty undergarments. It happens.

I've seen stretchmarks. (Do I have those there!? I will need to check when I get home.)

I've seen the dreaded cellulite under fluorescent lighting. Turns out that stuff is pretty common.

I've seen, or should I say witnessed, some of the worst deodorant fails, trapped in a tiny dressing room with very little air supply. Some deodorants just do not hold up very well.

I've dressed young brides.

I've dressed older brides.

I've dressed brides who could more than just fill out a gown. That zipper is not going any farther, trust me.

I've dressed brides who were so skinny and underweight that the dress had to be held together with a giant metal clamp so she could see what she might look like if she filled out.

I've even dressed the slightest little baby bump on a young girl who was worried that by the time she wore the dress, the little life inside her might take up more space in the gown than she was wanting to debut at her wedding.

I've seen the look of sticker shock on some brides' faces as they realized just how much that dress was going to cost.

I've also seen brides who thought the dress maybe wasn't expensive enough, and perhaps they could find a better designer gown somewhere else.

Then there were the brides who had actually done this whole thing before. This was not their first wedding dress! They often asked, "Should I wear ivory, or cream, or what about peach? Does that rule even apply anymore?" I didn't know the answer! I did know, however, to steer them away from choosing a peach wedding dress.

Sometimes the insecurities of the bride were so evident that it made the whole dressing experience awkward for them. Whether they were picking themselves apart physically over their appearance or they felt financially burdened over the cost of wedding planning, these brides did not always exhibit the joy of the day. On occasion, it was maybe even my own insecurity (guilty!) as I thought, *Why can't my hair be that thick and beautiful?* The comparison I always seem to succumb to—hair.

Here comes the fun part, though! The part we've all been waiting for. Once the bride was covered in the beautiful gown, that gown was the only thing you even saw. Stepping from behind the closed door of the dressing room, where all those flaws and imperfections had been uncovered and exposed, she would emerge beautiful and beaming with joy. I would be right behind her, carrying the sometimes long and heavy train, directing her to the platform, to be surrounded by multiple mirrors and softer lighting. Now the eyes of everyone in the whole boutique were on her, magnified. No matter who was in the store, anyone browsing would stop in their tracks. Oohs and aws would fill the entire place.

"What a beautiful dress!"

"Isn't she lovely!"

"Oh my ... that is so, so pretty!"

"Wow, stunning!"

Of course, the onlookers had not seen and experienced all the things that I had just witnessed back in the dressing room. The only thing they saw was the bride adorned in her beautiful wedding garments.

> I saw the holy city, the new Jerusalem, coming down out of heaven from God, prepared as the bride beautifully dressed for her husband. (Revelation 21:2 NIV)

Since my time as a bridal consultant—and later as a baker, making some beautiful cakes and getting to be behind the scenes setting up before the wedding— I've carried my experiences close at hand, never really knowing why I loved all things bridal. Weddings are just so exciting! I love how the Lord never forgot about my time there as well.

One day while I was in prayer, God heavily impressed upon me all those memories at once. As I prayed more, trying to figure out why they were flooding my mind, it became so clear. Clear as a wedding bell. He was giving me an illustration of how when we come to know Jesus as our personal Lord and Savior, it's a lot like stepping into the dressing room with Him. He sees all of us. He sees all our flaws. Don't we wish that our flaws were only physical ones? Because Jesus sees the deeper picture. Jesus sees our inward person. He sees our heart, our past, our guilt, our shame, our insecurity, our deep hurts, our traumas, our disappointments, our pride. Jesus sees our sin. He also sees past all those things. He is the Master Designer. He sees our potential—our joys, our compassions, and our future victories. Jesus sees the big picture. Just as the bridal consultant sees all of the bride in her imperfections and then helps her to become dressed in her bridal garments, that's what Jesus does for us.

When I thought of how the weddings of ancient Israel very much mirrored the fact that the church is the bride in waiting, I began to think like a bride. I began to prepare like a bride. We need to be preparing for when He comes for us at a moment's notice. Just as the bride had to have her lamp filled with oil in order to light her way, our lamp needs to be filled with God's Holy Spirit. When we take the initiative and actually read God's Word, and only then, we will get to know our Bridegroom Jesus beforehand, and we will recognize him when He arrives.

So, as He, Jesus, sits with us in the dressing rooms of our lives, we know He sees us fully. He sees all our imperfections and flaws, inside and out, and through his finished work on the cross, he redeems us. Jesus has pursued us and has offered to pay the bride price. He has offered his very own life in payment for us.

> Rather clothe yourselves with the Lord Jesus Christ, and do not think about gratifying the desires of the flesh. (Romans 13:14 NIV)

Go ahead and clothe yourself in His robes of righteousness. As individuals and in the body of Christ. He is in the dressing room with us. He will beautify us. He covers our sin. This transformation takes place when we get behind closed doors with Jesus.

> Behold, I stand at the door and knock. If anyone hears My voice and opens the door, I will come into him and dine with him and he with me. (Revelation 3:20 NIV)

He stands at the door knocking. If with a repentant heart we let Him come in, He will do the beautifying of our soul. Just as the Old Man, Adam, sinned, bringing death, the New Man, Jesus Christ, died for our sins, bringing us life. We don't want to ask Him into our hearts and then just go about living as the Old Man.

As we become the bride through this new relationship with Jesus, as it was with the brides of ancient Israel, so it is with us. We become the bride in waiting.

As brides in waiting, how can we be preparing to meet Him? I think one way is to find out all about Him through His Word. What does He like? What does He dislike? What pleases Him? How can we best love and pursue Him? Just as a bride knows whom she is marrying, we ought to know that we, the church, are marrying Jesus.

Earlier I mentioned that I was a very young bride by today's standards. There is something lovely about a young bride, but there are no age requirements to become the bride of Christ. Maybe you have acquired some years and are way past the age of a young bride, but Jesus is after our hearts. Our bridegroom, Jesus, pursues us just the same. We all need to be prepared for when Jesus comes back for us.

The Spirit and the bride say, "Come!"
(Revelation 22:17 NIV)

6

THE WEDDING BANQUET

When I think about the marriage supper of the Lamb, I can't help but think of all those who will be with us, from the friends and family who have gone on to be with the Lord, to all those saints of old from the Bible who were mentioned earlier. I can warmly picture my beloved grandparents, aunts, uncles, cousins, our precious little life lost through miscarriage, and most of all my mom and dad—all of them sitting around the table of the marriage supper of the Lamb, loving the company of Jesus.

My mom was especially known for setting the table when company came to dinner. She would make a remarkable presentation. it's a tradition that runs in her family. When I was young, I would watch her carefully dress the table, beginning with a beautiful tablecloth, freshly washed and ironed. She would have all the shiny gold or silver chargers, or red at Christmastime, placed under whatever beautiful china was chosen to suit the occasion. Next, she would pick out cloth napkins, folded in all sorts of creative and fun ways or wrapped with a lovely napkin ring. She would always place polished silverware in the correct order around the dishes. She wouldn't dare forget about the place card holders, with her guests' names beautifully handwritten. Elegant crystal stemware would stand tall to the right of each plate, ready to receive freshly brewed iced tea or water. Cups and saucers were in place and made to look cozy—we knew that my dad's special blended coffee would soon fill them up. To add the finishing touches, she would then light candles and embellish the table with centerpieces, lovely floral arrangements, usually carnations, simply placed in a delicate vase.

All of this together made every one of her guests feel so special as they found their names at her table, knowing that she had been expecting them. As soon as a prayer of thanksgiving was uttered, a delicious home-cooked meal followed, whether it be a savory baked ham with scalloped potatoes, a tender roast beef tenderloin with mashed potatoes and gravy, or a big pan of cheese-bubbling lasagna with garlic bread. Of course, a delicious dessert would end the meal: a cinnamon-filled apple pie, a decadent chocolate cake with vanilla ice cream, or an old-fashioned pumpkin pie, baked custardy and topped with homemade whipped cream.

The dinner conversation would be sweet, and laughter would be the main guest of honor.

I cannot think of more pleasant memories than sitting at my parents' table with cherished friends and family. I felt loved, accepted, and fully welcomed. I was supposed to be there. It was a place of safety, a place hidden away from the rest of the world. And if an earthly table can be so specially prepared and welcoming, can you just imagine how the table will be prepared in heaven by our Heavenly Father! He won't spare any details, like my mom's lavish table but with our Heavenly Father's touch instead. You too are supposed to be at this table. We are all invited.

> There is more than enough room in my father's home. If this were not so, would I have told you that I am going to prepare a place for you? (John14:2 NLT)

John the revelator describes this scene so beautifully in the book of Revelation.

> Then I heard something like the voice of a great multitude and like the sound of mighty peals of thunder, saying, "Hallelujah! For the Lord our God, the Almighty reigns. Let us rejoice and be glad and give the glory to Him, for the marriage of the Lamb has come and His bride has made herself ready." It

was given to her to clothe herself in fine linen, bright and clean; for the fine linen is the righteous act of the saints. Then he said to me, "Write, Blessed are those who are invited to the marriage supper of the lamb.'" And he said to me, "these are the true words of God." (Revelation 19:6–9 NASB)

7

THE BRIDEGROOM COMES

There's a traditional song that is played at weddings as the bride walks down the aisle. You can hum the chorus now! You know the one, *dum-dum-de-dum, dum-dum-da-dum*. Well, now just replace one thing: here comes the groom! Yes, our Bridegroom, Jesus, is coming.

Years ago, I attended a young friend's wedding and was so very excited to see her as a bride walking down the aisle. She was a naturally beautiful person, but everyone knew that as a bride adorned in her bridal apparel, she'd be especially beautiful. As the wedding procession began and the anticipation built, the bridesmaids and groomsmen all proceeded down the aisle. Next, there they were, the bride and her father, standing in the archway, ready to slowly proceed down the aisle. Sure enough, she was as stunning as expected. All eyes were on her, ready to watch her every step down that aisle.

But just before they took that first step, I felt a sense of urgency to direct my attention toward the groom. I thought, "What! Look at the groom? No, this is the bride's big moment!" But I did it. I reluctantly turned my attention toward the groom—and was amazed at what I saw! As the groom gazed upon his bride, a look of awe covered his face. He looked as if he had waited his whole life for this moment, As if he was already exclaiming, "I do, I do, I do!" As the bride slowly glided closer, it was as if he wanted to leap off the altar, run to greet her halfway, scoop her up into his arms, and carry her the rest of the way.

I immediately thought about Jesus, my special Bridegroom. As tears welled up in my eyes, It occurred to me right then that the Holy Spirit was giving me a clear picture of what is to come in regard to the church. Because of this, I now have become one of those people who cry at weddings. And at every wedding I have attended since then, I now always look at the groom's reaction while everyone else is gazing at the bride. It is a perfect reminder of how Jesus, our Bridegroom, affectionately looks upon His bride with such great anticipation to be with her.

This life is so fleeting. Our time on this earth is very short, in light of eternity. One definite thing about this life is that it has its ups and its downs, its hills and its valleys. Although life is certainly a beautiful, precious gift to be lived out with thankfulness, it can also be touched with great loss, sorrow, and sin.

Remember that evil serpent back in the garden? Well, he is still the enemy of our souls today. He is the one who introduced death. He is still trying to make sin look attractive to our human eye, just as that delicious fruit looked to Adam and Eve. They thought that fruit would fill them up, only to find themselves left empty, as sin often does. The enemy of our souls is relentless, and he does not fight fair. He does not take any days off. The Bible says,

> Be sober, be vigilant; because your adversary the devil walks about like a roaring lion, seeking whom he may devour. (1 Peter 5:8 NKJV)

Jesus Himself said,

> These things I have spoken to you, that in me you have peace. In this world you will have trouble; but be of good cheer, I have overcome the world. (John 16:33 NKJV)

Jesus most certainly has overcome the world.

The wedding plans are in order. The table for the banquet is being set now. The good news is that we have all received an invitation to this banquet! Every one of us. And not just to attend as guests; most important, we get to be the bride.

He is coming back for His bride. Be ready, lovely bride. Here comes the Groom!

Printed in the United States
by Baker & Taylor Publisher Services